STEM Superstars

Lonnie Johnson

by Rachel Castro

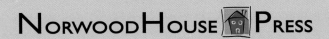
NORWOOD HOUSE PRESS

Cover: Johnson talks about his inventions.

Norwood House Press
Chicago, Illinois

For information regarding Norwood House Press, please visit our website at:
www.norwoodhousepress.com or call 866-565-2900.

Hardcover ISBN: 978-1-68450-924-9
Paperback ISBN: 978-1-68404-456-6

Library of Congress Cataloging-in-Publication Data
Names: Castro, Rachel, author.
Title: Lonnie Johnson / by Rachel Castro.
Description: Chicago, Illinois : Norwood House Press, [2020] | Series: STEM superstars | Audience: K to grade 3. | Includes bibliographical references and index.
Identifiers: LCCN 2018054268 (print) | LCCN 2018058297 (ebook) | ISBN 9781684044610 (ebook) | ISBN 9781684509249 (hardcover) | ISBN 9781684044566 (paperback)
Subjects: LCSH: Johnson, Lonnie, 1949---Biography. | African American inventors--Alabama--Biography--Juvenile literature. | Inventors--United States--Biography--Juvenile literature. | African Americans--Alabama--Biography--Juvenile literature. | LCGFT: Biographies.
Classification: LCC T40.J585 (ebook) | LCC T40.J585 C37 2020 (print) | DDC 338.7/68872 [B] --dc23
LC record available at https://lccn.loc.gov/2018054268
319N–072019
Manufactured in the United States of America in North Mankato, Minnesota.

★ Table of Contents ★

Chapter 1

Growing Up

Lonnie Johnson was born in Mobile, Alabama, in 1949. His father was a truck driver. His mother was a nurse's aide.

Johnson grew up and attended school in Mobile, Alabama.

5

Building his own toys led Johnson to inventing and science.

Johnson's father taught him how to build his own toys. Johnson wanted to be an **inventor**.

Did You Know?

Johnson had five brothers and sisters.

One day he tore open his sister's doll. He wanted to see what made its eyes close. He also tried to make rocket fuel in his family's kitchen. He almost burned down the house!

Johnson liked rockets at a young age.

Chapter 2

Science and School

Johnson entered a science fair in school. He made a **robot**. Johnson spent one year building it. It was more than three feet (1 m) tall.

Children today still like to make robots for science projects.

At a science fair, judges look at every project.

The contest was at a university. Johnson was the only black student there. Some people would not talk to him. The judges did. He won the contest.

Johnson's high school was
segregated. Black kids had to
go there because of their race.
He graduated in 1969. He went to
Tuskegee University.

Schools used to be segregated by race.

Chapter 3

Working and Inventing

Johnson worked as an engineer at NASA. He designed spacecraft. They went to Jupiter, Saturn, and Mars.

Johnson worked on the *Cassini* probe mission to Saturn.

Johnson invented the Super Soaker. It started as a water pump. When he tested it, it shot water. He thought it could be a toy.

Early Super Soakers were simple toys.

20

The first Super Soakers were sold in 1990. Kids everywhere wanted one. Kids still play with these toys. And Johnson is still inventing today.

Johnson holds his invention, the Super Soaker.

★ Career Connections ★

1 Try making your own toys. If you don't know where to start, take apart a toy car or clock with an adult to see how it works.

2 Visit a space museum to learn about space and the probes that explore it.

3 Your library may have free science-related programs for youth. Ask a librarian to help you find a club or after-school program to join that interests you.

4 Enter your school's science fair or ask a teacher about local science contests.

5 Johnson studied engineering in college. He took many math and science courses. Ask an adult about what math and science courses you can take.

★ Glossary ★

engineer (en-juh-NIHR): A person who designs, builds, and improves products or machines.

inventor (in-VEHN-tor): A person who is the first to think of or make something.

NASA (NASS-uh): National Aeronautics and Space Administration, an American agency that is responsible for air and space technology.

robot (ROH-bot): A machine that can perform actions instead of a human.

segregated (SEG-ruh-gated): Separated from others, especially because of race.

★ For More Information ★

Books

Chris Barton. *Whoosh!: Lonnie Johnson's Super-Soaking Stream of Inventions*. Watertown, MA: Charlesbridge, 2016.
This book teaches readers more about Lonnie Johnson.

Quinn M. Arnold. *Mars*. Mankato, MN: Creative Education, 2018.
This book helps readers get to know what makes Mars special.

Websites

Johnson Education: STEM Opportunities for Students
(https://www.nasa.gov/offices/education/centers/johnson/student-activities/index.html) This page contains information on how students can talk with real astronauts and videos of interviews.

Toy Hall of Fame: Super Soaker
(http://www.toyhalloffame.org/toys/super-soaker) This page shows photos of early Super Soakers and talks about the history of the toy.

★ Index ★

★ About the Author ★

Rachel Castro is a Minneapolis-based writer. She holds degrees in English literature and creative nonfiction. In addition to writing for the educational market, she works for a public library and teaches creative writing.